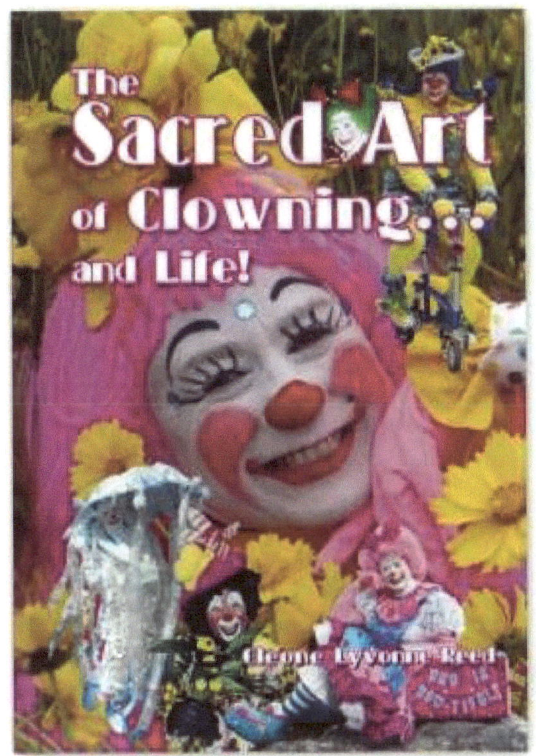

Author of The Sacred Art of Clowning... and Life!
Cleone Lyvonne Reed, Clown for over 26 years
has ALL of her clown clothes, props...
EVERYTHING for sale in one huge bulk purchase!

cleonelreed@gmail.com
541-999-6125

Visit https://www.blurb.com/b/9506212-i-ve-got-a-dream

Examples of the clown wardrobe: men, women, children, all sizes. Pictured here are many of Cleone's students from different states and countries, different nationalities.

See the variety in Cleone's clown wardrobe. Pictured here: Cleone's husband's family, Cleone's friends, and Cleone as Pistachio, Lulu, Chloe, and Ms. Ninnie Poopski.

Chloe's Wardrobe	$5,170
LuLu's Wardrobe	$ 695
Ms. Ninnie Poopski's Wardrobe	$2,395
Professor Wanda B. TATI's Wardrobe	$ 895
Pistachio's Wardrobe	$ 395
TOTAL Cleone Reed wore as a clown:	$9,550
Wardrobe for Men	$2,190
Wardrobe for Students	$1,340
Accessories and Props	$2,276
TOTAL Cleone's Clown Closet:	$15,356
Wimzie's Costume	$2,995
GRAND TOTAL	**$18,351**

TOTAL PRICE OF EVERYTHING LISTED IS

$18,351

(Clown: $15,356 + Wimzie: $2,995)

NO INDIVIDUAL SALES

(With the possible exception of the Wimzie Costume)

Entire Lot Sold As Is to SOLO BUYER/COMPANY/CORPORATION

Visit https://www.blurb.com/b/9506212-i-ve-got-a-dream

Quite a few little additions/surprises will be thrown in,

such as clown stilts, balloons, makeup, etc.

A Week to Train a Troupe of Clowns is a Negotiable Option.

Cleone made her debut May 15, 1994. The shoes are one of a kind that she made to match this ensemble.

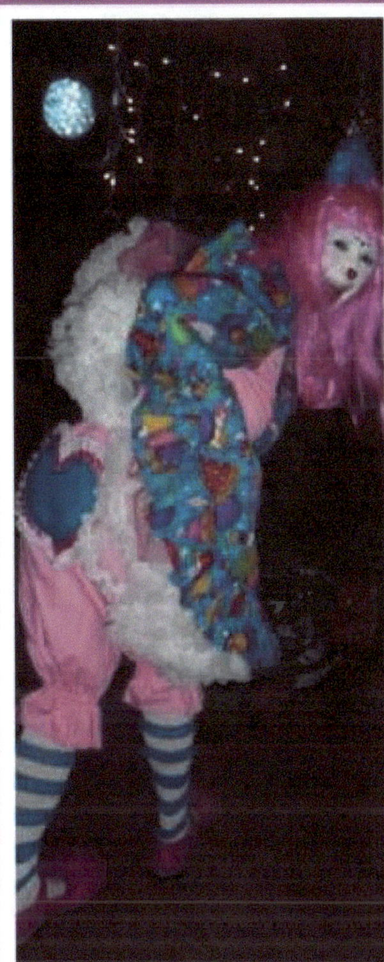  

PARTY print: Skirt with ruffle and appliqued bib, pink blouse with party print sleeves, pink bloomers with satin heart on the butt, party print bow for the hair, big bow on the back of the skirt.
Shoes & wig not included.

VALUE: $595.00

Notice the PARTY outfit goes with both her home-made shoes

and the pink leather shoes.

Again, a variety of wigs or shoes goes with this versatile ensemble of blouse, reversible vest, skirt, bloomers, cuffs for both ankles and wrists, and shorts.

Rainbow skirt
with matching blouse
with butterfly appliques.

Floral bloomers.

Orange ruffle and
headpiece to match.

Orange shoes
with flowers
to match headpiece.

VALUE: $695.00

Wig and socks
sold separately.

A famous clown instructor (Mark Renfro) at Clown Camp at the University of Wisconsin brought Cleone up in front of an audience using her as an example of ingenious costume design matching her headpiece with her decorated oversized shoes.

Let Me Call You Sweetheart

The most fabulous blouse ever with ruffled sleeves, a ruffled skirt, matching bloomers and matching bibbed reversible pants. Ellie the stuffed elephant, two headpieces, and over-sized red shoes with hearts.
Includes a foam camera that pops out a tennis ball on fishline that acts as a flash bulb. Great prop for a parade.

Most exquisitely sewn professional ensemble ever!

Wigs only thing not included.

VALUE: $995.00

Dress up or wear pants! Surprise people with this awesome camera prop,

or discover where Ellie, the stuffed elephant, has her music buttons!

Jellybeans, clowns, ruffles galore!

This bibbed lined skirt with ruffles galore and matching blouse with puffy and ruffled sleeves comes with matching hairbow, ankle cuffs, neck ruffle, clown socks, petticoats, Easter hat, and a purple yarn wig.

Clowns are popular in parades, and riding in a borrowed golf cart or a fun car makes it easier if anyone has limited mobility.

Let it Snow

Models: Peanuts, Pistachio, and Pecan

Most of what you see here is available to outfit two Holiday clowns, except the shoes on the two ends.

Wigs not included.

VALUE: $395.00

This is a very comfortable outfit that can be worn as a clown . . .

Or when not in clown, just to be festive for the holidays.

LuLu loves snakes, frogs, cows, pigs, and sunflowers!

Cut-off Farmer's overalls have patch pockets and all the things LuLu loves appliqued or sticking out of her pockets. Sunflower petals collar, wrist and ankle cuffs, blue braided wig, hat with sunflowers, yellow shirt, yellow tights, and green shoes with sunflowers to match her hat.

Also included: LuLu's toys (frog puppet, frog hugger, etc. AND her little clown bike!!!

VALUE: $695.00

This clown outfit is an all-time favorite, especially when clowning with children. LuLu entertained in a neighborhood in La Paz, Mexico, that had no electricity or running water, a real major highlight of Cleone's clowning career.

TATI's wardrobe: reversible pants and reversible jacket with pockets, bib with ruffle, buttons, and bow; reversible jumpsuit, blouse, hair bows, graduation cap, and long pink wig. Yellow striped clown socks. Pink professional leather clown shoes.

VALUE: $895

Professor Wanda B. TATI clowned in Faial (an Island in the Azores/Portugal).

This outfit packs really small but plays big and is great for traveling.

Ms. Ninnie Poopski, "The Life of the Potty," advocates for good colon health.
Her "identity and name" and entire wardrobe and all her props for sale as a set!
Plaid dress and collar and wrist cuffs, hat with dragonfly, reversible cape,
polk-a-dot dress, and dress with "Life of the Potty" appliqued on it.
Props include a flush toilet, "Poopsie's Colon Cleanser," a stethoscope
with a toilet plunger on it, a teeny tiny "stool sample," and so much more.
Includes yellow leather shoes.   VALUE: $2,395.00

Ideally, someone will manifest the goal of this clown and get connected with a product or organization to inspire people in our country to have better colon health! That is what gives this collection value. If JUST the clothes, the value is half what is stated here.

Reversible tuxedo jacket with long tails and reversible pants with pockets on both sides. Includes a turtleneck (either red or green). Wigs not included.

VALUE: $895.00

Three different men wore this attire for parades and is one of Cleone's favorite creations. The tuxedo jacket is reversible, but the side with alphabet squares always won out!

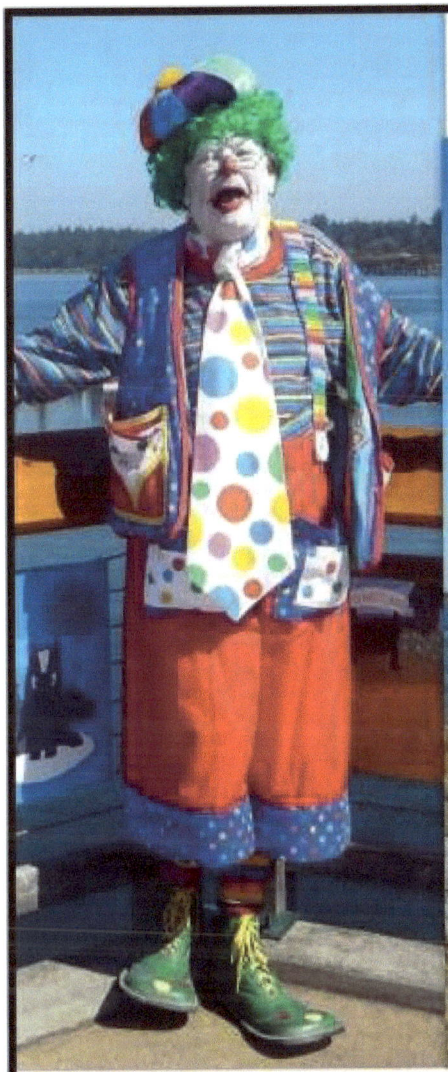

Pants with suspenders and
a hula-hoop in the waistband.
A reversible vest.

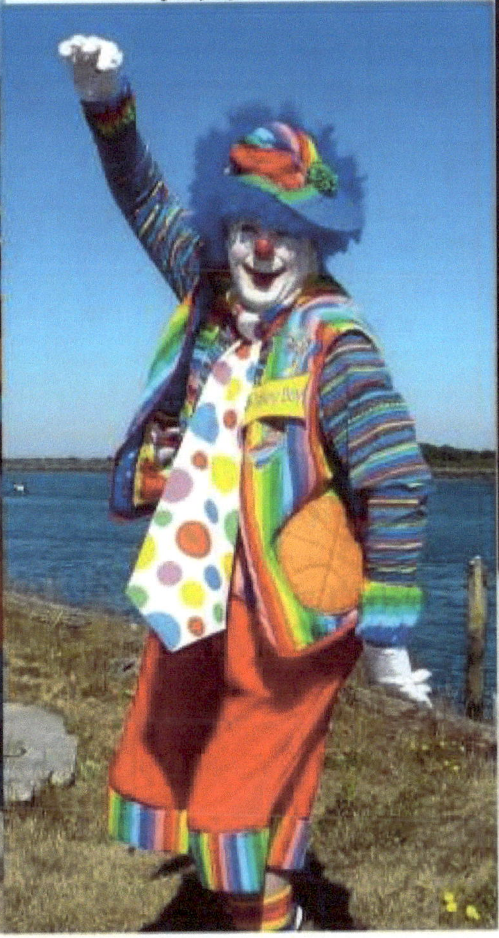

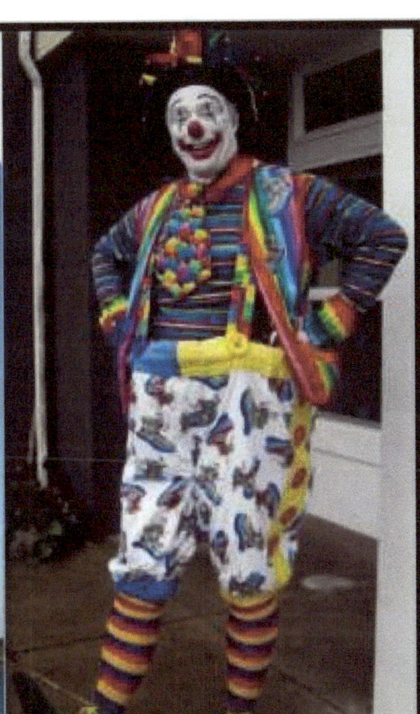

Reversible red pants.
Reversible clown cuffs.
Striped shirt.
Two clown ties.
Three clown hats.
Clown socks.
Professional green
leather shoes worth
$300.00!

SIX DIFFERENT COMBINATIONS
with the two pants and reversible vest.
Plus change things up with the
variety of hats and two ties.

Value: $1,295.00

Wigs sold separately.

So many variations, a unisex ensemble, but most often this was worn by men.

There

may be

many

more

surprises

for

children,

including

an outfit

for an

infant!!

*For a musical clown
of slight build.*

The chest plate with the musical staff
is removable from the top.
The billowy pants feature pockets
with musical symbols appliques.
Includes clown socks.

Professional
$300 leather jester
shoes complement
this musical ensemble.

VALUE: $695.00

This musical clown's name was Gentello, a magnificent mellow fellow.

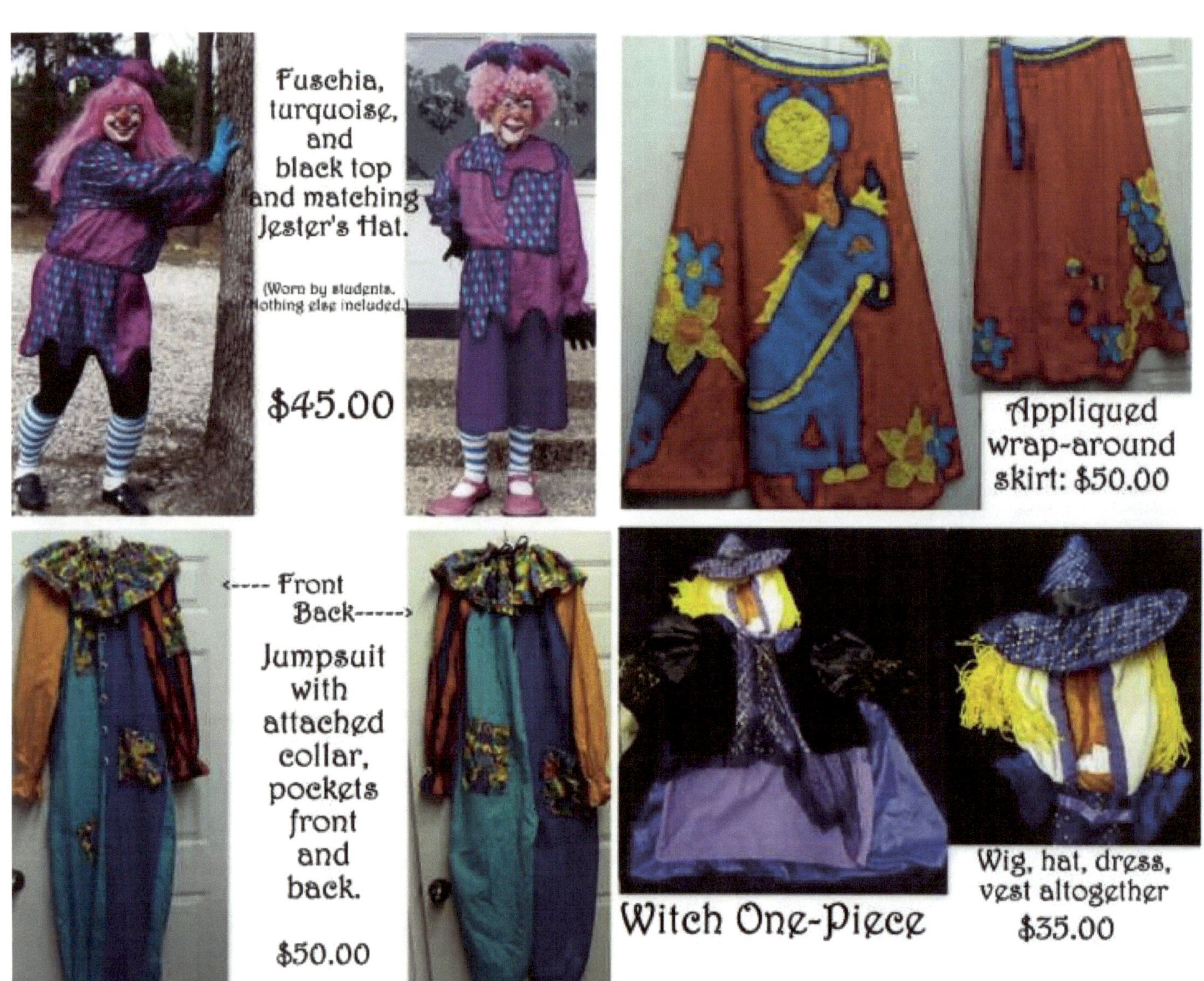

Here are a few of the clothes students wore at weekend workshops.

A striped clown one-piece with patch pockets used by 3 students.
Yellow neck ruffle, head pieces and candy bead necklaces included.
VALUE: $195

It was wonderful having something a tall man could wear
or women who were overweight and not easy to fit.
These clowns were all comfortable in this one-piece outfit.

Candy Corn Jumpsuit for Halloween

Yellow blouse with ruffle and ruffled cuffs goes under candy corn jumpsuit. Add double candy corn ruffle with rick rack trim, put on either the candy corn witch's hat or the pumpkin hair band (or both). And top it all off with a double-breasted blazer if you're cold!

VALUE: $145.00

Only once a year, but perfect for that one special night!

Wimzie was the main star on a television program called "Wimzie's House" in Canada in 1995-96. This walk-about costume is the real deal, made for the program by Costume Specialists in Ohio. Wimzie is a "dragon/bird hybrid with yellow-orange skin, purple hair tied in pigtails with baby blue bows and red wing-like antlers on the top of her head. Fits most average-size adults between 5'2" and 5'8". Retail Value is $3,000.00 plus. Make any event special with Wimzie and be ready for children to line up to have their picture taken with Wimzie. NOTE: This is not a fat person inside. The costume is constructed to make her look this shape, so anyone wearing it will look like this. She is absolutely adorable. Like brand new. Absolutely no wear or tear. VALUE: $2995.00

A VERY UNIQUE COSTUME!

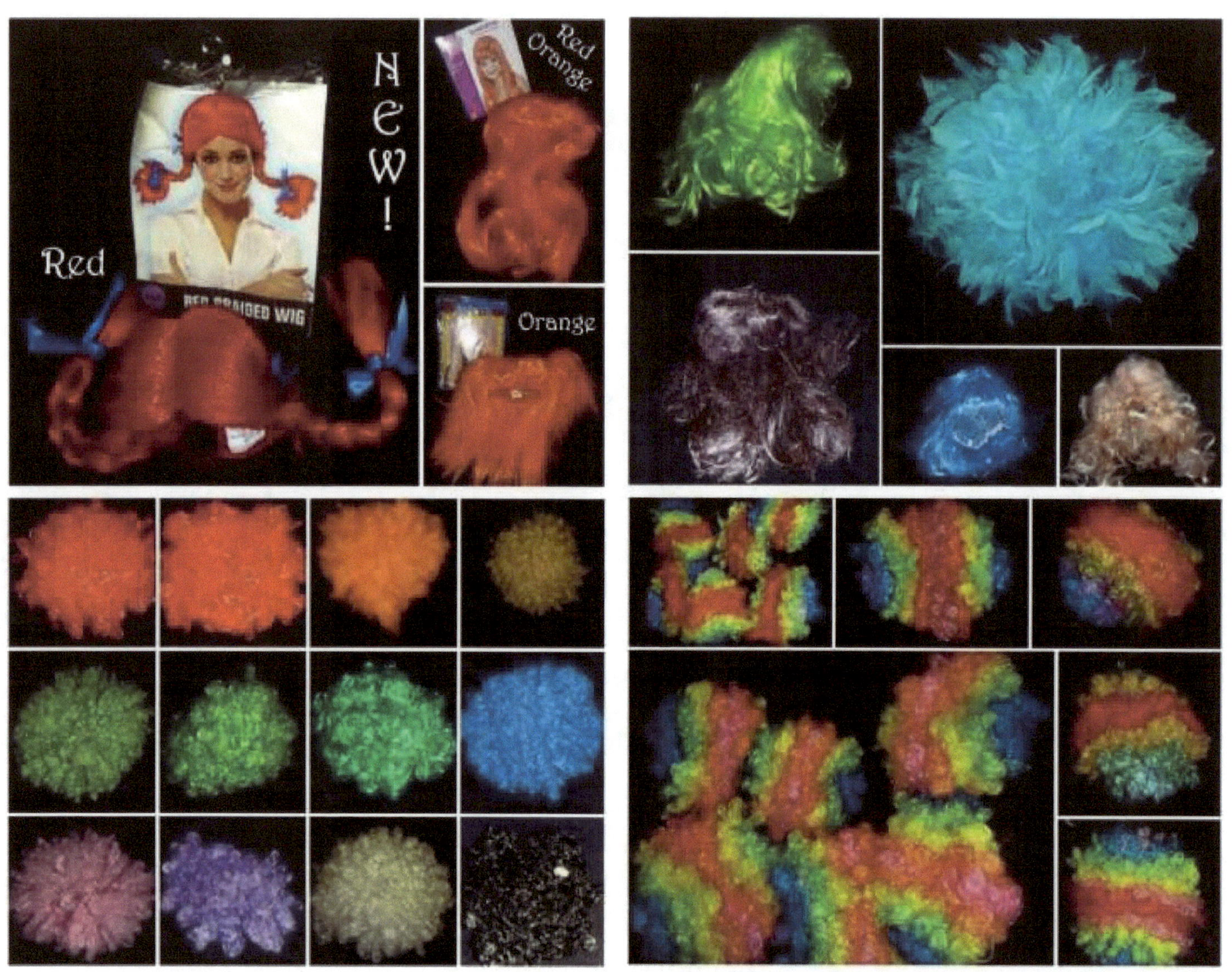

NEW WIGS, $25.00; Specialty Wigs, $20.00; Curly wigs, $15.00; Rainbow Wigs, $10.00
Value: $515.00

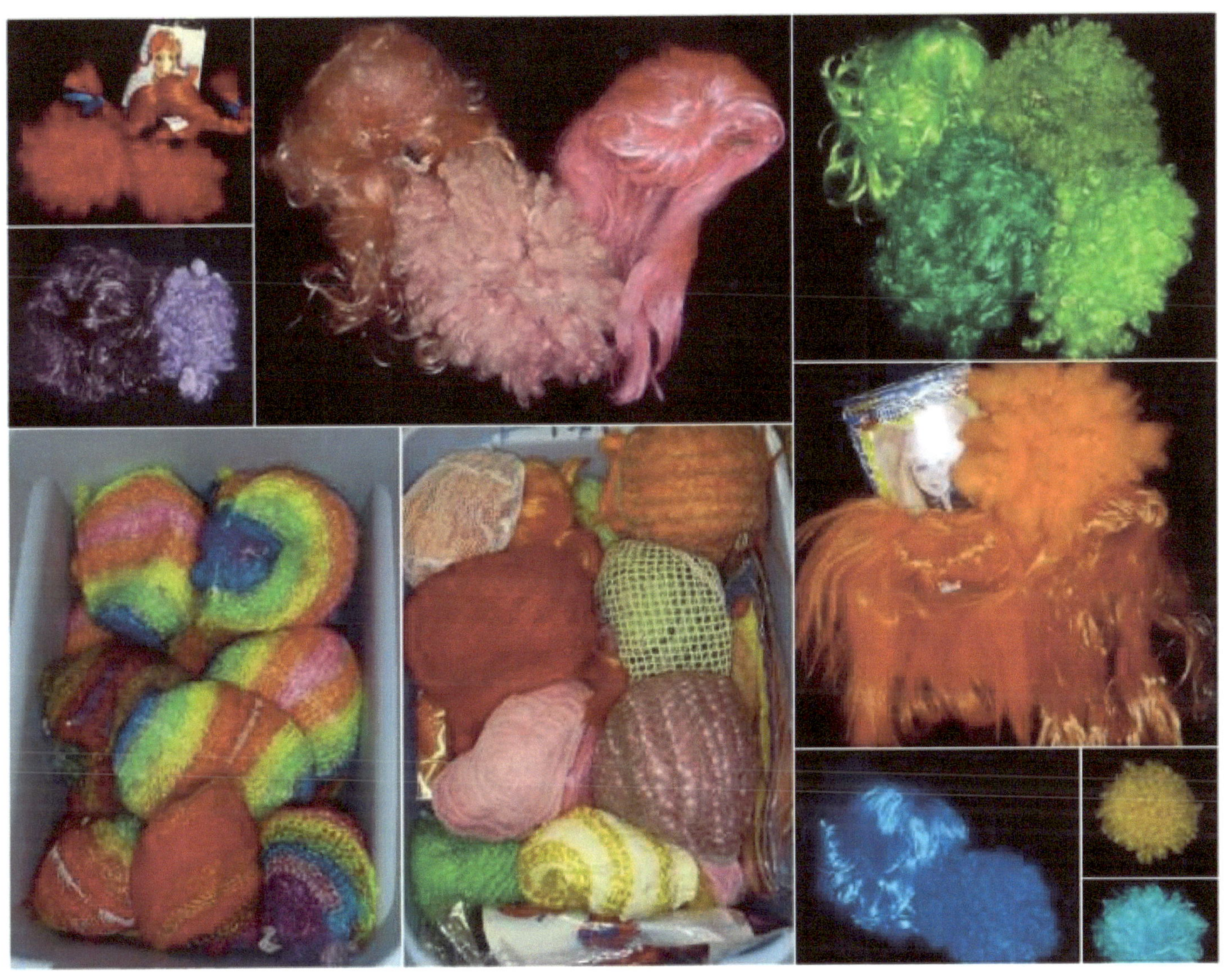

Another way to look at them, in color combinations and how they are stored in a bin.

Bird hat FABULOUS ($45.00). Rooster and chicken hat ($25.00 each).
Crab hat ($20.00), Ears and tails, (each set $15.00), Reindeer headband ($10.00),
and the Rainbow headband ($25.00). Total value: $180.00

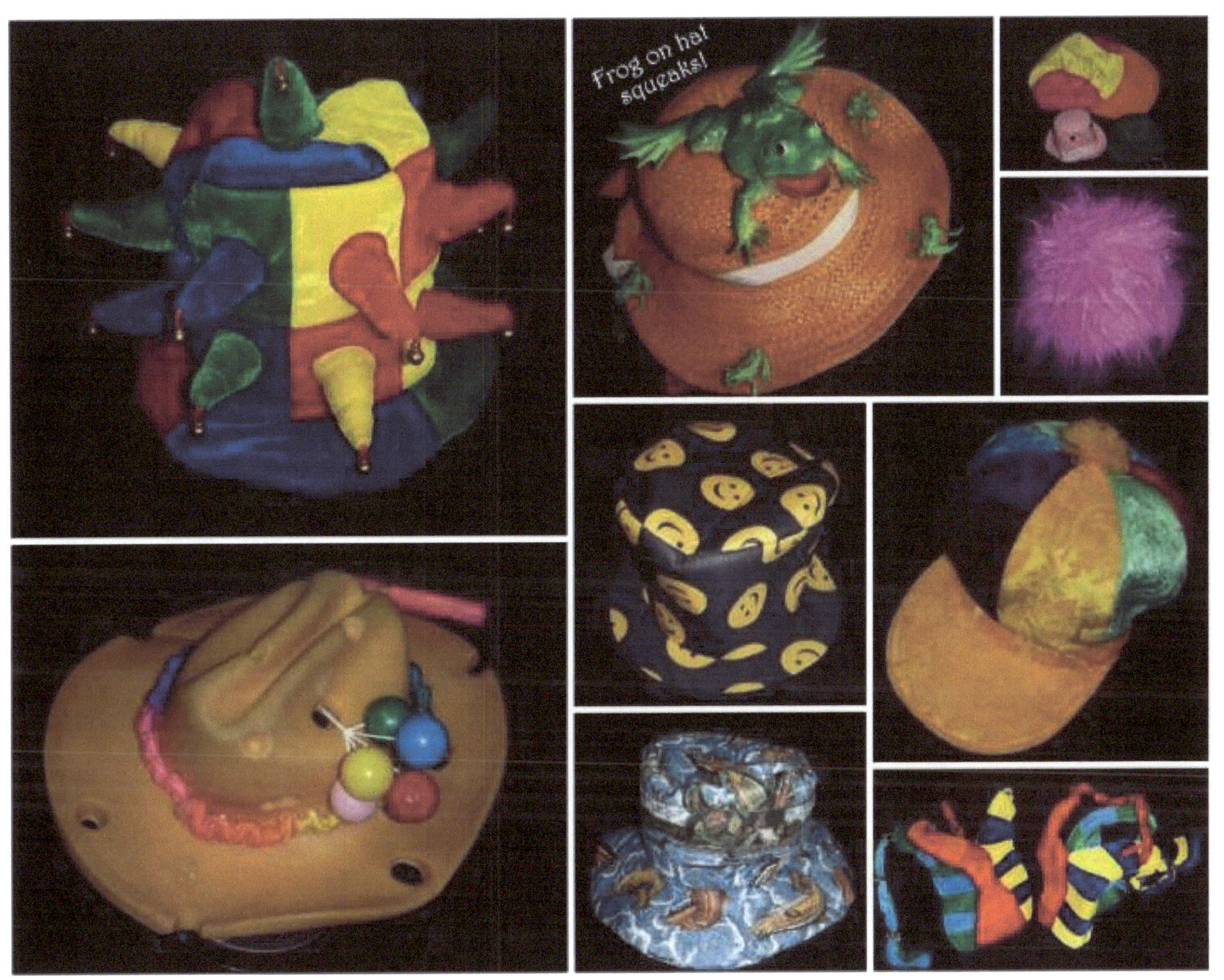

Great hats, some home-made, some purchased.
Total value: $195.00

My favorite headbands for parties, weddings, any special events, sometimes for clowning. Just really fun feminine stuff! All for $200.00.

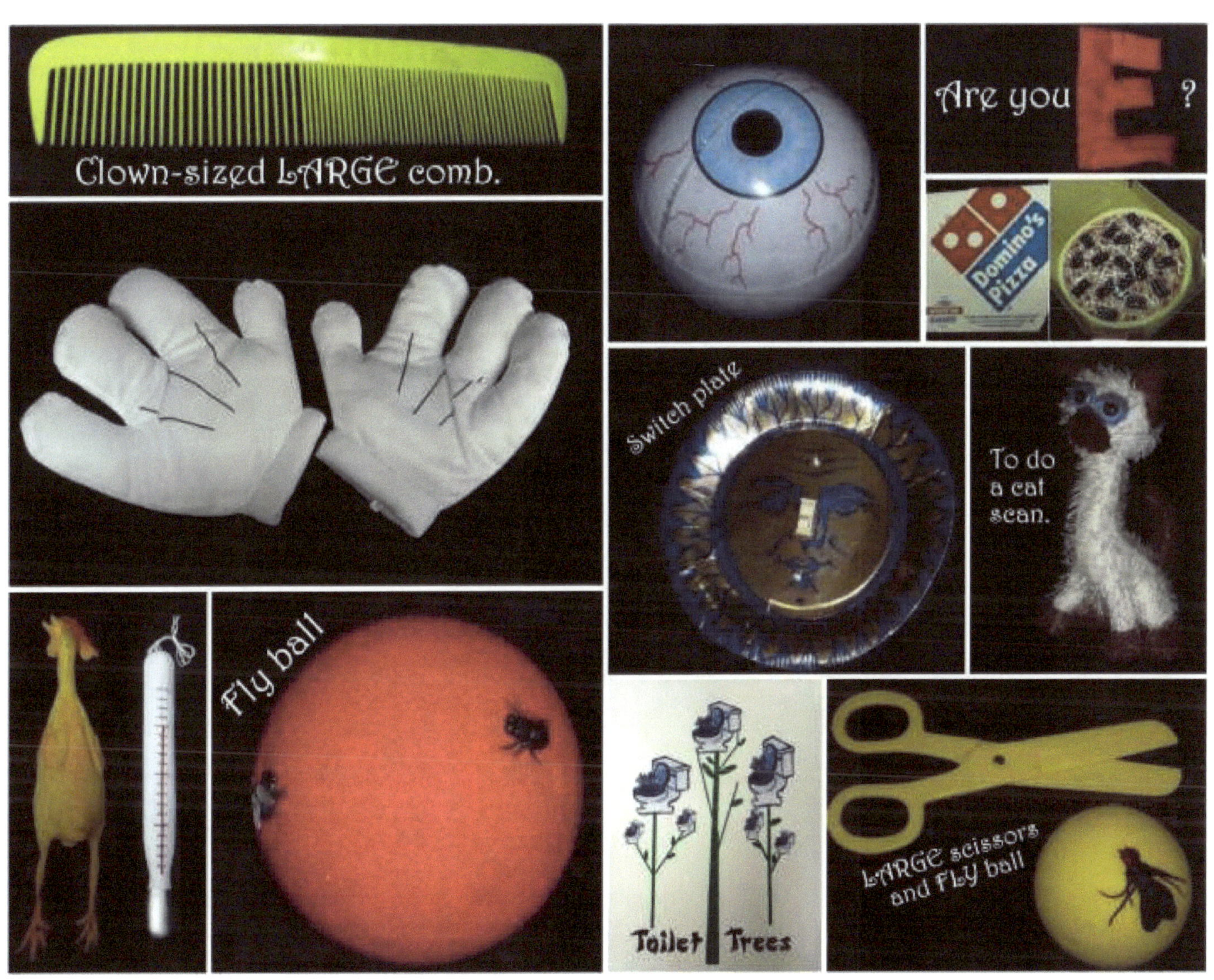

A box of props and puns.

TOTAL VALUE: $95.00

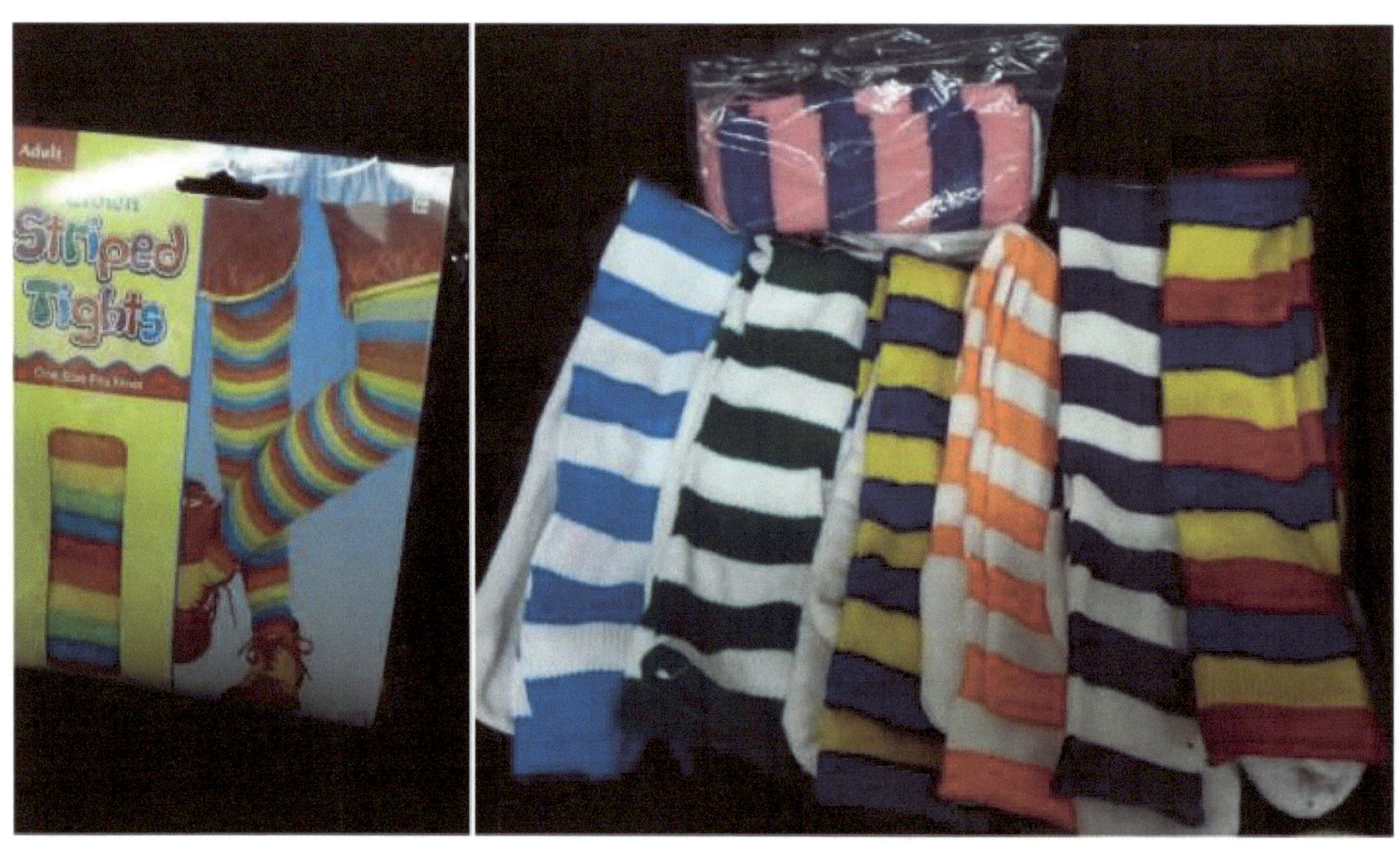

These socks and tights mix and match with several of the outfits.

Value of the clown collection: $1006

These can be given away in orphanages, hospitals, nursing homes, etc.

O. Oh-Yes Clown
T. Two Black Clowns
R. Big-Horn Clown
H. Clown clock
J. Clown Rock
V. Thinking Clown
D. Clown with Parasol
E. Glass clown on bike with balloon
P. Pom-Pom Clown
Q. Golf Hobo Clown
U. Clown Bust
X. and W. Musical Globes
Y. Dottie Musical Clown
Z. Zeke Clown
$20 each or two for $30.00
BB. Switchplate Clown
GG. Clown Troll Doll
HH. Set of Chloe Mugs (2)
$10 for the set
FF. LuLu Magnet
EE. Crying Clown

Two sets of appliqued clown towels: 2 bath, 2 hand, 2 washclothes AND a new floor rug: VALUE: $85.00

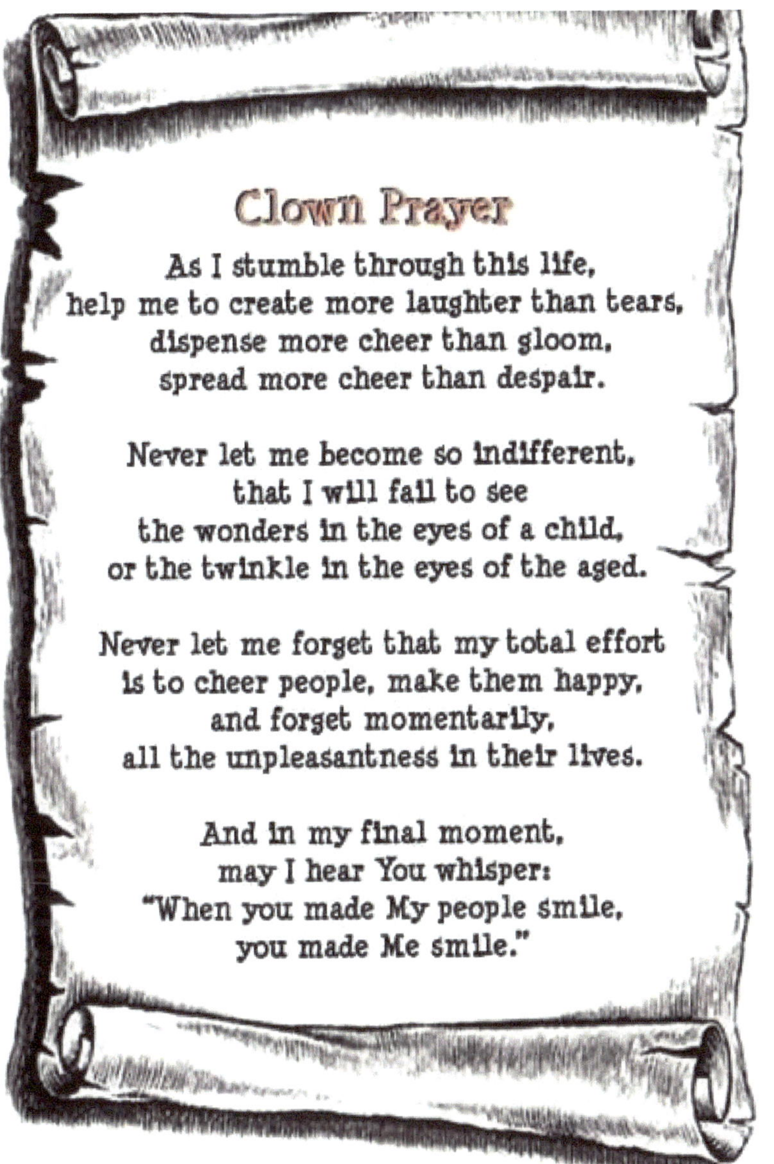

Reviews about Cleone's book, *The Sacred Art of Clowning... and Life!* are presented on the following pages to illustrate the energy in this collection of clown clothes, props, etc.

Caring clowning is about love. All of Cleone's clowns are beautiful, not scary. She made almost all of the clothing featured in this book. The Clown Prayer here captures it all.

REVIEWS OF MY BOOK ON AMAZON

5.0 out of 5 stars
Clowning Is No Joke
By Malcolm Kushner on, January 17, 2012

Part memoir, part how-to, and part inspiration, *The Sacred Art of Clowning* as a whole is greater than the sum of its parts. And its parts are pretty darn good. Clowning has come a long way since the days when it was just a bunch of people coming out of a car in a circus. Over the past 20 years, clowning has become more associated with hospitals than three-ring entertainment. It is now central to the humor and health movement. And Cleone Lyvonne Reed's journey reflects that trend.

Her book describes how she has used clowning to cope with difficulties in her own life, as well as brighten the lives of others. You will be inspired. You will be enchanted. And you may even want to take up clowning yourself. (You'll find plenty of ideas for doing so.) But if you want to follow in the author's footsteps, remember one thing. You'll have big shoes to fill—clown shoes. And that's no joke.

The Sacred Art of Clowning... and Life!

Cleone Lyvonne Reed © 2012

ISBN: 978-1-934759-57-8
CATEGORY: Memoir/Clown Education/Psychology
6 x 9 paperback, 182 pages, $14.95
Available through www.blurb.com, Amazon.com,
and rdrpublishers.com as a paperback or eBook

5.0 out of 5 stars
The Therapeutic Power of Putting on the Red Nose

By Richard R. Blake, VINE VOICE, on January 6, 2012

Reading ***The Sacred Art of Clowning...and Life!*** is a refreshing uplifting experience. I am enthused by the new way of thinking Cleone Lyvonne Reed introduces in her book. Cleone skillfully weaves selected memoirs of her own "transformational journey from abuse to bliss" as she describes the mission and therapeutic benefits of clowning and the sacredness of clowning as an art form.

As in any art form each individual reader will take away their own personal impressions of the impact and intent of the author's message. I came away with an awesome sense of the importance of finding beauty in life and in the individual person. I identified with the sense of SACRED whether in "Clowning or in Life," and enjoyed Cleone's use of alliteration in creating an acrostic in developing much of her material.

The clown pictures created by Illustrator Richard Vergara add uniquely powerful visual reinforcement to the applications of each of the "Twelve Universal Powers" introduced in Part Three. Clowning encourages living outside the box, empowerment, authenticity, creativity, and gives birth to passion. I also appreciated the insightful and motivational quotations included throughout the narrative. The colorful cover and dozens of photographs of clown creations and events immediately captured my attention. I perused the book in it's entirely before settling in to a most pleasurable read.

Reed's writing is transparent, engaging and highly motivating. As an avid reader I explore a broad spectrum of topics. I may read to acquire information, to be entertained, as a brief escape, or for motivation and inspiration. While reading ***The Sacred Art of Clowning...and Life!*** I became totally immersed in Cleone's Caring Clown Character Creations.

5.0 out of 5 stars
Awesome book

By Shelley on January 18, 2012

Read the book the day I got it. Loved it! Really enjoyed how the author described caring clowns and the work that goes into clowning, creativity, empathy, enthusiasm! Also loved the pictures. Hope all care givers read it; laughter is the best medicine!

5.0 out of 5 stars
Read This Book Slowly to Absorb It's Impact.
By David W. Magidson on, June 11, 2012

Cleone asked me to review her book a few months ago. I don't know her, we've never met, never even talked on the phone. She found me by way of my blog and my resume. My blog is boswickclown. blogspot.com, (if you're curious who I am); I write for professional children's entertainers. I'm a former Ringling Brothers clown and have been training and performing for 25 years. To me clowning is an art and a science.

This book took me a long time to read; it made me think and think... I keep the book by my night stand and read it as a source of inspiration.

I was afraid of this book when I was asked to review it. I'm an atheist but spiritual. I've seen far too many Christian Clowns that hide behind their message as an excuse for not being good or funny. I'm generally wary of clown books.

Cleone reveals so much about herself and her journey as a person and a clown. It's a beautiful book; she GETS clowning. She and I have so much invested emotion in clowning, I would often read a passage in this book and turn the book over to think about what she just said. Clowning is never about your pretty costume, how many clubs you can juggle, what a wonderful balloon you make; it's about connection with your audience and making people laugh. **As a clown and a writer she invites us in to be hugged.**

It's wonderful how Cleone talks about visiting a hospital or a senior center and sometimes just making physical contact with another human. Tossing out what you had "planned" is clowning. Sometimes bringing overwhelming comic love into a place is clowning. Being present and learning from one moment to the next, that's what Cleone writes about.

I think this is a beautiful book, written from the heart. It's the kind of book you can flip open to any section, read, and get something new every time.

The role of a clown and a physician
are the same —
it's to elevate the possible
and to relieve suffering.
~ Patch Adams

Cleone Reed and Patch Adams

* 9 7 9 8 5 5 6 6 8 4 7 3 7 *